Emotional Intelligence
in a week

JILL DANN

Hodder & Stoughton

A MEMBER OF THE HODDER HEADLINE GROUP

Orders: please contact Bookpoint Ltd, 130 Milton Park, Abingdon, Oxon
OX14 4SB.
Telephone: (44) 01235 827720, Fax: (44) 01235 400454. Lines are open from
9.00–6.00, Monday to Saturday, with a 24 hour message answering service.
Email address: orders@bookpoint.co.uk

British Library Cataloguing in Publication Data
A catalogue record for this title is available from The British Library

ISBN 0 340 849703

First published 2001
Impression number   10 9 8 7 6 5 4 3 2 1
Year   2007 2006 2005 2004 2003 2002

Typeset by SX Composing DTP, Rayleigh, Essex.
Printed in Great Britain for Hodder & Stoughton Educational, a division of
Hodder Headline Plc, 338 Euston Road, London NW1 3BH by
Cox & Wyman Ltd, Reading, Berkshire.

The leading organisation for professional management

As the champion of management, the Chartered Management Institute shapes and supports the managers of tomorrow. By sharing intelligent insights and setting standards in management development, the Institute helps to deliver results in a dynamic world.

Setting and raising standards

The Institute is a nationally accredited organisation, responsible for setting standards in management and recognising excellence through the award of professional qualifications.

Encouraging development, improving performance

The Institute has a vast range of development programmes, qualifications, information resources and career guidance to help managers and their organisations meet new challenges in a fast-changing environment.

Shaping opinion

With in-depth research and regular policy surveys of its 91,000 individual members and 520 corporate members, the Chartered Management Institute has a deep understanding of the key issues. Its view is informed, intelligent and respected.

For more information call 01536 204222 or visit www.managers.org.uk

CONTENTS

Introduction		5
Sunday	Overview of EI and EQ	9
Monday	Becoming more self-aware	22
Tuesday	Generating an Internal Observer	33
Wednesday	Stress management and EI	47
Thursday	What will my company gain from an investment in EI?	60
Friday	How to create an EI culture	73
Saturday	Preparing for the next developmental steps	86

Experts are beginning to agree that types of intelligence other than IQ (Intelligence Quotient) have evolved in humans over the last two million years. A high IQ is not enough to guarantee success in life. When you have a high EQ (Emotional Intelligence Quotient) you are adept at interpreting the emotional roots of your own thinking and behaviours and *choosing* your actions to influence outcomes. You are also capable of making good insights into the behaviours and reactions of others.

What is Emotional Intelligence?

We think and act on emotions stimulated by the present environment and past events, in accordance with our life script. Since much of brain function is still being researched, Emotional Intelligence is one form of intelligence that we are discovering or beginning to understand.

Put simply, EI is an intelligence distinct from intellectual intelligence (e.g. the purely cognitive, innate capacities measured by your IQ). Intellectual and Emotional Intelligence derive from different parts of the brain and so they function in different ways. Your EQ is complementary to IQ, because it concerns the perception and processing of emotions.

There are views of intelligence, which distinguish gifted individuals in mathematics, music, artistic ability, management and technology. EI describes abilities distinct from these more academic or intellectual intelligences.

Intellect (cognition or thinking) is based on the workings of the Cerebral Cortex (3rd Brain), the more recently evolved layers at the top of the brain. Emotions are controlled by the more ancient Subcortex (2nd Brain), a lower part of the brain.

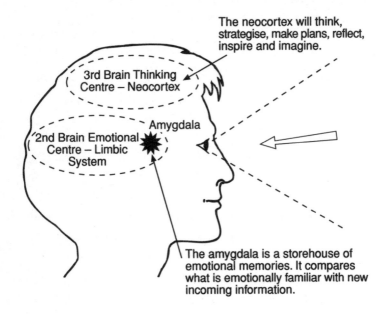

The neocortex will think, strategise, make plans, reflect, inspire and imagine.

3rd Brain Thinking Centre – Neocortex

Amygdala

2nd Brain Emotional Centre – Limbic System

The amygdala is a storehouse of emotional memories. It compares what is emotionally familiar with new incoming information.

For many leading companies in the UK, Emotional Intelligence (EI) has become the core of soft skills competencies and management development.

The Emotionally Intelligent manager

- Is self-aware, motivated and perceives others accurately
- Manages emotions to create well-formed outcomes
- Is emotionally literate, recognising underlying blanket emotions

- Prepares for people interactions by looking at the psychological process as well as the task
- Thinks positively, is authentic, clears things up and does not easily quit if a difficult conversation is required
- Has increased flexibility, able to let go of out-of-date visions and plans
- Proactively creates a life/work balance, has excellent social skills and sense of community
- Is resilient when the going gets tough, seeks solutions
- Seeks personal development without a sense of personal deficit.

Whereas IQ is more or less a given, EQ can be learned. The distinction is about your way of *being* not of *doing*. Improvement cannot be achieved solely by attending a training course or reading a book to acquire knowledge.

There is no single view of what EI is; there are a number of different views (as with many management topics). Daniel Goleman, one well-known author, defines EI as:

The capacity for recognising our own feelings and those of others, for motivating ourselves, and for managing emotions well in ourselves and in our relationships.

When people are handled badly businesses lose money through wasting time. Equally, effectiveness can be improved by mastering relationship skills with customers, suppliers and staff. Leadership requires excellent EI competencies, which can have a startling effect on personal and business success. This might seem a tall order, but it can be achieved through increased EI.

■ I N T R O D U C T I O N ■

This book looks at the main areas that EI touches in everyday life and in business life.

The week ahead comprises:

Sunday	Overview of EI and EQ
Monday	Becoming more self-aware
Tuesday	Generating an Internal Observer
Wednesday	Stress management and EI
Thursday	What will my company gain from an investment in EI?
Friday	How to create an EI culture
Saturday	Preparing for the next developmental steps

Overview of EI and EQ

Today, we are going to gain an understanding of:

- History of EI
- Measurement of EQ
- Benefits of Emotional Fitness
- EI is learnable
- When you get emotionally hijacked
- How will it change me?
- Keeping a journal.

History of EI

EI is not new. Is it just another management fad? Let's hope not. EI provides us with a framework for bringing emotions to the workplace. But where has EI come from?

The concept of EI has been around for some time in one form of another.

Year	Originator	EI related concept
1920	Thorndike	'social intelligence'
1935	Doll	'social competence'
1940	Wechsler	'nonintellective intelligence'
1948	Leeper	'emotional thought'
1966	Leuner	'emotional intelligence'
1973	Sifneos	'alexithymia' (cognitive-affective deficits)
1983	Gardner	'personal intelligences'

1983	Sternberg	'practical intelligences'
1985	Bar-On	'EQ'
1989	Saarni	'emotional competency'
1990	Salovey & Mayer	'emotional intelligence'
1994	Bagby & Taylor	'TAS (Toronto Alexithymia Scale)
1995	Goleman	'Emotional Intelligence'
1996	Dulewicz & Higgs	'IQ, EQ and MQ'
2001	Dann	'Emotional Fitness' exploring use in primary and secondary health care and Syndrome X patients

References can be found on the internet for all of the above.

Measurement of EQ

A number of different EI Assessments or 'tests' have been developed. The core proposition is the same; you can develop better self-awareness, self-regulation and the ability to use your senses to enhance your health, success in relationships or to influence others.

Assessment gives individuals information about their own competence either through self-scoring or through 360° instruments (reverse appraisal of managers, feedback from peers as well as seniors). The main EI schools of thought are:

- The Bar-On Emotional Quotient Inventory (EQ-i™ – Dr Reuven, Bar-On and Dr Steven Stein
- The Emotional Competence Inventory (ECI) – Boyatzis, Goleman and Hay/McBer
- The EQ Map™ – Advanced Intelligence Technologies and Essi Systems, Orioli, Robert K Cooper and Ayman Sawaf
- The Emotional Intelligence Questionnaire (EIQ™) – Dulewicz and Higgs through ASE
- The Multifactor Emotional Intelligence Scale (MEIS™) and the Mayer, Salovey and Caruso EI Test (MSCEIT™)
- HeartMath Europe – Hunter Kane Limited.

You will find two assessments in the book *Test Your Emotional Intelligence* (Hodder & Stoughton) if you want a taster for the process and others on the internet, if you use the search engines. My recommendation is that the reader should focus on development and not become hooked on measurement alone. However, it is useful to have an assessment at the start of EI development and one about a year into it.

To determine why EI is important and should be a development priority, we need to look at the personal case for doing so. EI is backed up by a great deal of data and research (see *Test Your Emotional Intelligence* for an overview).

Benefits of emotional fitness

Over the last two decades, many people have tackled their physical fitness and taken charge of their diet to establish a good life balance. People who go to fitness centres, gyms and health spas are generally goal-oriented and want to be more effective. Many people join clubs to feel or look better, follow a beauty regime and to help control their stress. Some have investigated alternative therapies to reduce the impact of stress in their lives. How many have concluded that these are the only solutions to a balanced and healthy life?

Many people stop exercising because they 'lose motivation'. Having to spend 30–40 minutes practising relaxation techniques to wind down at the end of a busy day is very time-consuming. If this is on top of a beauty regime and the gym three or four times a week, it is even more protracted. However, if you are constantly looking after your emotional fitness, it is unnecessary to have to relax to recover from turmoil at work and in your personal life. Prevention is better than cure – always!

The benefits to you of implementing the EI development in this book, combined with practical guidance on physical fitness are:

- Gaining an understanding of how EI can help to maintain motivation, beneficial brain chemistry and well being
- Improving your interpersonal skills and relationship success by acquiring knowledge, insight and increasing self-awareness. You can apply this to generate energy and vitality in the face of pressures at work and in your home
- Gaining an understanding of how to reduce the 'post-event' effort to relax as well as support stress management strategies that reduce the likelihood of long-term illness
- Becoming equipped with the basic skills to deconstruct your own behaviour in areas where it is mystifying or

unhelpful, and to generate foresight rather than hindsight about your behaviour
- Gaining an understanding of the mind-body link and those factors that contribute to your emotional well-being.

Through a combination of the above, you can generate a new way of being in the 21st Century and save yourself some time.

EI is learnable

Raising EQ is possible because EI is learnable. Modern neuroscience tells us that the emotional centre of the brain learns differently to the cognitive centre. We can learn to fine-tune, or increase our use of, different parts of the human brain.

Remember what it was like when you first learned to drive a car? You did not know what you did not know. Do you remember how the way you were treated affected your ability to retain the lessons and your self-confidence? Alternatively, do you remember changing cars and having to retrain yourself to switch on the lights without having to think where the switch was? Getting to do these things at the 'unconscious competence' level involves building a new neural pathway in your brain.

You will know if you need to find out more about how you learn best. What ways of learning do you find most helpful? If you do not know how to explore your learning preferences I suggest that you set up a period of enquiry. Your preferred learning style (Kolb, David A 1984 Experiential Learning, Prentice-Hall) may be to engage in immediate activity rather than pausing to reflect. We will cover this activity on Saturday.

Learning ladder rung number	What it feels like when you are on it
1 Unconscious incompetence	You do not know what you do not know
2 Conscious incompetence	You now know what you do not know and you may not like it
3 Conscious competence	You know what you know and feel clumsy practising this new-found knowledge or skill
4 Unconscious competence	You feel as if you have always known this or been proficient in this skill

Two types of learning

If you are really in tune with your needs, you will find it easier to tackle the kind of learning involved in raising your EQ. We have postulated that there are two basic types of learning:

- **Cognitive.** Cognitive learning is about absorbing new data and gaining of insights into existing frameworks of association. We also need to engage that part of the brain where our emotional signature is stored. Changing habits, such as learning to approach people positively rather than avoiding them or to give them feedback skillfully, is much more challenging than simply adding new data to old.

- **Emotional.** Emotional learning involves this and more. Emotional learning involves new ways of thinking and acting that are more in tune with our identity – our values and beliefs and attitudes. If you are told to learn a new word processing program, you will probably get on with it; however, if you are told that you need to improve control of your temper, you are likely to be upset or offended. The prospect of needing to develop greater emotional intelligence is likely to generate resistance to change.

When you get emotionally hijacked

Consider this. You've had a long and exhausting day visiting some stunning country on holiday. You arrive back to enjoy an excellent meal, but retire early and fall into a deep sleep. Suddenly wide awake, you sit bolt upright to be confronted with a tiger so close that all you can see are its eyes. You have an immediate and very strong emotional reaction which causes you to do one of three things (and maybe some others too!):

1 you freeze; or
2 you leap out of bed and run like mad; or
3 you throw something at the offending animal.

You have just experienced an amygdala highjack: Freeze, Flight or Fight. Early humans relied on this reaction for their survival when confronted with danger. If Darwin is correct, we are the progeny of those ancestors who utilised the reaction successfully and survived, unlike the rest who did not.

Let's look at what happened. Your reaction is an instantaneous adrenaline-based reaction and has no cognition associated with it. It is an emotional hijack because the 2nd Brain processes reactions some 80,000 times faster than the Neocortex processes thoughts (3rd Brain).

How can we take advantage of this faster processing? The greater speed is beneficial when we use it to make better decisions using wide-ranging sources of data: soft (emotional, intuitive) information as well as the traditional hard (cognitive, knowledge) data. It is powerful when we pick up information from all our senses and use it more perceptively to manage physiology, relationships and social situations.

'The ancient brain centers for emotion also harbor the skills needed for managing ourselves effectively and for social adeptness. Thus these skills are grounded in our evolutionary heritage for survival and adaptation.'

Daniel Goleman's *Working with Emotional Intelligence* (1998).

Implications in a business environment
In summary, to survive we developed a reaction that was appropriate to the situations that Early People encountered when physically threatened. Let's consider the inappropriateness of this response in modern business. You are likely to have had several close-call situations causing an adrenaline-rush. When the boss says, 'I want to see you in my office in 5 minutes', do we carefully consider all of the reasons why? No, we immediately assume we are in trouble and panic.

Your body is primed for action and is reacting with the fight reactions of anger, aggression and hostility or the flight/freeze emotions of fear, anxiety and nervousness. It is stressful not to be able to release the fight or flight energy provided, through expected physical activity. This lack of release causes many illnesses.

Today, there are generally fewer threats to our personal safety. The main threats that we perceive are of a financial,

emotional, mental and social nature. These types of threats are not generally dealt with immediately.

How will it change me?

You may feel better mentally and physically, but it would also be perfectly normal to relapse back into some unhelpful behaviour. However, you would have better information about the lapse and be able to prevent a recurrence. People might say that you look less stressed or that you do not overreact and you may feel more grown up and happier.

Symptoms of low EQ

- We are worried, anxious and confused about priorities
- We are time-pressured, inefficient, and perform poorly
- We are tired, fatigued and frustrated
- We have a poor work–life balance
- We may have elevated blood pressure
- We age more quickly.

Keeping a journal

Raising your EQ to reduce and eliminate unproductive behaviour is rarely completed in one step. Development of any kind is difficult with low self-awareness; something which is notoriously difficult to train. It has to be part of a developmental process over a period of time, usually following a pattern of input, reflection and discovery.

I recommend that you start a journal that we will use throughout the week and conclude on Saturday. The idea is to consistently log your learning, to make this as easy as possible and to keep the information in one place, readily to hand. Keeping the journal will allow you to prepare for meetings – noting your feelings, thoughts or expectations of the event.

Making a record while the memory is fresh will give you the benefit of higher quality reflection. Stick to keeping the journal; it takes three weeks to form a good habit. I keep a single book including my work notes as well. At least once a year, I review the content, tabbing up the pages. I write up my conclusions, plus any follow-up activity in my latest journal. Often I find little gems of advice that I missed.

If you use the following format with some academic rigour, you might be able to include the material as part of a suitable qualification (such as management or organisational development).

Journal format
The journal chronicles the steps on the route. General rules are to:

- Date the entry, giving qualitative details of the environment and experience
- Give some context (why, where and with whom). Give anything relevant about the timing, such as an appraisal interview
- Note anything that distracts you (you may be participating in a meeting, listening to a presentation or giving a coaching session, etc)
- Note anything that interferes with your relationship(s) with other participants and with your role (chairperson, coach, etc).

I am going to give you voluntary exercises designed to deepen your understanding throughout and at the end of each day. We recommend that you experience EI development before making any judgements about its use. You have to *feel* the difference between Emotionally Intelligent behaviour and undeveloped behaviour.

Most managers I have worked with say it is only when they look back that they can distinguish their former way of being around people.

Activity: the cost of low EQ

Think for a moment of three examples where you had a strong emotional response to how you were handled:

- In a face-to-face encounter as a customer with a supplier (such as with a shop assistant)
- By e-mail or through a telephone conversation

- Using CTI (Computer Telephony Integration) to access a service.

Write down in your journal the emotions you experienced and if there were any flashbacks to previous experiences:

- How did you respond to or behave towards them?
- How did you feel afterwards?
- Was there any further action or reaction (e.g. a letter of praise or complaint)?

In the next chapter I ask you to explore your own awareness. If your immediate response to this is that you are too busy and this request is irrelevant to your life, then I entreat you to question your priorities.

Discover the power of *now*.

Becoming more self-aware

Today, we are going to gain an understanding of the
following topics:

- What is self-awareness?
- The importance of emotions
- Raising self-awareness
- Self-awareness competencies
- Journal entries and activities

What is self-awareness?

The sages said, 'the world is right here – all we have to do is
to empty our minds and open ourselves to receive it'.
Consider, for a moment that your mind is preoccupied with
the 'busyness' of your life. A lifetime of doing and achieving.

Do you live in the here and now? How self-aware are you?
There are arguably three levels of awareness:

- Awareness of the outside world – what you now see, hear, smell, taste and touch
- Awareness of the inside world – physical sensations such as neck ache, seating pressure points, the feel of your skin in your clothes and the emotions that come to you in your stream of consciousness
- Awareness of fantasy activity – all cerebral and limbic system activity beyond the present 'here and now'. Things that you feel, think and even emulate or simulate, but are not actually part of the here and now.

You may imagine yourself to be both strong and deeply in
tune with your feelings, aware of others' emotions and adept
at social intercourse to further your ambitions. Alternatively,
you may feel that you are living a script written by someone
else and that you are not in control of the outcomes in your
daily life.

If you have low self-awareness, the main learning outcome
for you is to simplify your life by consistently recognising
distinctions between reality (what actually happened or is
happening) and fantasy (interpretation of what happened,
your preferred outcome or projection of what may happen in
the future). Most people 'daydream' about things they would
like to happen or they recycle past events and create
alternative outcomes.

'Heart and head combined

It is very important to understand that EI is not the opposite of intelligence, it is not the triumph of head over heart – it is the unique intersection of both. Emotional Intelligence combines emotion with intelligence . . .

. . . In this view, emotion and thinking work together: emotion assists thinking, and thinking can be used to analyse emotion. EI then is the ability to use your emotions to help solve problems and live a more effective life . . .

. . . Emotions are nagging thoughts. Emotions are very often unwelcome guests in our lives. Yet, emotions provide us with information, which if ignored, can cause serious problems. If we are aware of our emotions, if we act on our emotions in a rational way, then we will increase the odds in our favour.'

Mayer & Salovey, Chicago EI Conference paper, September 1999

The importance of emotions

Before the benefits of high EQ can be grasped, the bedrock of EI is acknowledgement of the importance of emotions in business as well as personal life.

> The importance of emotions
>
> - our bodies communicate with us and others to tell us what we need
> - the better our communication, the better we feel
> - emotions help us establish our boundaries
> - emotions have the potential to unite and connect us
> - emotions can serve as our inner moral and ethical compass
> - emotions are essential for good decision-making.

Look at the suggested importance of emotions and log what you think and feel in your journal. If you have problems distinguishing thoughts from emotions, delay doing the exercise until you have read Tuesday. You may like to share the reflection and debate with a friend or colleague.

Raising self-awareness

Take a few moments to think of examples where you show heightened self-awareness and where you showed more limited awareness. I recommend that you write this down in your journal.

> The impact of increasing self-awareness
>
> Self-awareness means that we are aware of what we think and feel in the present. If you developed your EI, starting with increased self-awareness, what effect would it have:
>
> - at home?
> - in life?
> - at work?

Common examples of heightened self-awareness would be:

- becoming aware of your present driving style and the impact it is having on other motorists
- being aware that you feel uncomfortable around a person, although not necessarily being aware why
- repeating a pattern of unhelpful behaviour; being aware you are starting down a well-worn path and are unable to stop it. Write down at least two instances of the same pattern and we will use this tomorrow.

Your learning curve from self-awareness to social adeptness
- To be self-aware you need to be emotionally literate. The next step is to be able to distinguish and label accurately individual emotions (see Tuesday). Then on to become increasingly capable of self-control regardless of the emotions triggered by a situation.
- You then learn to increase your choices of behaviour in given situations. You can go on developmentally to use this to become more aware of others, their triggers and the emotional roots of their unhelpful behaviours.
- Finally, as you choose to develop, you become very socially adept using your self-awareness, self-regulation and awareness of others.
- You may elect to go on further acquiring knowledge about different cultures and customs. A goal may be to manage your reaction to unexpected clashes in moral, ethical and sociocultural standards.

When you become self-aware and emotionally literate, you are able to distinguish single emotions triggered unexpectedly by some event. This can help you become aware of a personal boundary (what you can take and what you cannot endure). You then need to decide what to do with this insight to look after your emotional needs.

Emotions can serve as our inner moral and ethical compass – tuning in precisely can help us with problem solving. Sometimes employing purely analytical approaches using rational weightings does not serve us well. We need both rational and irrational information.

Emotions are essential for good decision-making – businesses are now beginning to accept that gut feeling and instinct has its place in making sound business decisions. Similarly in our private lives, when it comes to selecting a lifestyle option, the balance of advantages should include satisfying unmet emotional needs.

Create a list of times when you are out of sorts and you do not perform as you would like in terms of being self-assured. Treat this as a list of things that you choose to complete to eradicate your self-doubt. It could be that you write down items that cause you to be under-confident due to issues such as:

- Relationships
- Misconceptions
- Unchecked assumptions about people or events
- Upsets.

Become aware if your lack of confidence allows you to avoid being accountable or to procrastinate. Catch yourself in the act. If you defer decisions, make yourself think it through, write down the pros and cons. Write down who is impacted and how they would feel. Are you showing a lack of respect for others? Is that what you really want to happen – people to feel disrespected by you? Realise the consequences of your lack of self-belief. This may help you to motivate yourself to eradicate negative beliefs (see *Neuro-Linguistic Programming in a week*).

- Are you letting down others by doubting your self-worth and capabilities?
- Are you playing the victim?

Self-awareness competencies

My personal view of what it takes to be self-aware is summarised in the following boxed list.

Self-awareness competencies

Awareness of Feelings: Recognising one's emotions and their effects. People with this competence:
- ❏ know which emotions they are feeling, can name why and label them
- ❏ realise the chain from emotion to action (links between their feelings and what they think, do and say)
- ❏ recognise how their feelings affect their performance, the quality of experience at work and in relationships
- ❏ have a guiding awareness of their values or goals and any gap between espoused values and actual behaviour.

Personal Insight: Knowing one's key strengths and frailty. People with this competence are:
- ❏ aware of their strengths, weaknesses and emotional boundaries in relationships
- ❏ reflective, understanding the power of learning from experience even if reflection is not their natural style
- ❏ open to candid feedback, new perspectives, continuous learning and self-development

---

❑ objective about feedback from others and able to generate positive strokes for themselves appropriately

❑ able to show a sense of humour and perspective about themselves.

Self-assurance: Sureness about one's self-worth and capabilities. People with this competence:

❑ present themselves with self-assurance; have 'poise' with warmth

❑ can celebrate diversity in teams, voice views that are unpopular and go out on a limb for what is right

❑ are decisive, able to make sound judgements using emotional and cognitive information despite uncertainties (perceptions of risk) and pressures

❑ are generally recognised as self-confident

We feel powerful when our communication is congruent and aligned inwardly. Conversely, when communication breaks down we are preoccupied and unable to concentrate on other things.

Exercise – self-awareness competencies

Note the answers to the following in your journal.
- Which of the above competencies do you feel represent your strengths?
- Why?
- How do you feel about those competencies?

How would you practice and develop them:

❑ at home?

❑ in life?

❑ at work?

Journal entries

Reflect on the following examples from my life:

Create a log in your journal.

Consider a life of being present in the 'here and now', experiencing distinct emotions, being able to label each one and to track where they came from in the past. Does it make you fearful? Does it call on your cynicism for protection? The most outstanding things are achieved by *being* differently about them – much more so than by *doing* anything differently.

When I have put myself under extreme pressure, say, changing from a perfectly successful career in the Royal Navy to a life of self-employed peaks and troughs, the only thing that has got me through is my degree of self-awareness in any one situation. I have been aware before, during and after the key events in all three aspects of consciousness. I have used the third level of awareness, the fantasy element:

- to prepare for any meetings or interviews
- to visualise or simulate how the others present may be projecting my performance at the time, based on my answers to questions
- to predict how the first few days of an assignment may be.

The other two levels of the outside and inside worlds have been about managing my responses and my posture, tonality, stance, presentation (attitude) and so on.

Developing self-awareness takes you to another level of being.

What relevance does EI have to me?
The start of self-awareness is to test your readiness to change.
Have you any motivation to change?

Tick all that apply. Developing your EQ will help you if you
are concerned with:

❑ your influencing skills; wanting to understand others more
   in terms of what persuades them, what they can actively
   listen to and really hear
❑ stressful situations that get on top of you and that cause
   you to be anxious about them hours after they have
   occurred or which wake you up in the middle of the night
❑ getting the message across to people unambiguously and
   being able to listen without inner dialogue disrupting
   concentration
❑ your life–work balance because it must become more
   equitable and you need to renegotiate how your time is
   spent

❑ relationships that are stressful or even mystifying in terms of your behaviour or the reactions of others
❑ your general health being below what is accepted as a healthy norm and suspecting that it is self-inflicted injury in the form of bad habits, self-deprecation and lack of commitment.

Log in your journal any conclusions you reach about why EI is of interest or of use to you from the above list and your own ideas. Leave space to log more conclusions as they occur to you throughout the week. Plan your next step for raising your EI competencies using this feedback.

While it only takes a short time to read each chapter, it should take you some time to run through all of the exercises. If you hesitate over this as a priority, ask someone that you trust about the personal case for you doing so.

Tomorrow, we will look at building on self-awareness by increasing our self-control through the use of our inner voice.

Generating an internal observer

Today, we are going to gain an understanding of the
following topics:

- Understanding the ABC model
- Deconstructing and rebuilding reactions
- Taking control of your behavioural patterns
- Becoming emotionally literate
- Recognising blanket emotions
- Moving from hindsight to foresight
- Competencies for self-control
- Journal entries

Understanding and using the ABC Model (Affect, Behaviour & Cognition)

Before you can really get a grasp on why it is worth using EI
as an approach for personal development and systemic
culture changes in business, we need to go through some
events in slow motion using the ABC model (Affect,
Behaviour & Cognition). The following A⇒C⇒B happens in
seconds.

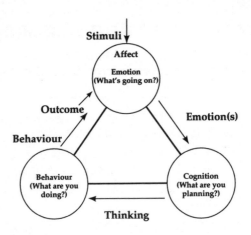

The model should be referred to as the ACB model as the flow is from emotion (<u>A</u>ffect) to thought processes (<u>C</u>ognition) resulting in observed activity (<u>B</u>ehaviour).

Deconstructing and rebuilding reactions

Humans experience a number of feelings at the same time or experience them as a chain of emotions. Behavioural patterns are actions that you tend to do over and over in response to a particular situation. For example, when you get angry you shout, when impatient you may tap a pen on the table or swing your foot back and forth.

It is important to learn to distinguish emotions to get more information about what is driving you. Do you have any patterns of repeated behaviour that do not make sense to you? Most people have some bad habits that they know do them no good.

Just as our thoughts are tied in with our emotions so our behaviour is also tied in. Tracking back through these provides powerful insights to repeated unhelpful behaviours.

We need to become aware of a potential negative emotional reaction before we act on it. During or in the immediate aftermath of unhelpful behaviour we need to take note of the emotions that triggered it. By deconstruction, we come to understand why things occur repeatedly. You have to be able to intervene in your own thinking to be able to break bad habits.

You need to pick up the emotions generated by given situations and work out where they came from. We learn the stimuli so that when they are next triggered, we intervene and choose another behaviour or opt not to respond (i.e. just forget about it).

Remembering the diagram of the brain centres from the Introduction:

- *Hindsight* (initially) comes from the 2nd Brain. Reflecting on the outcome, considering the effect and the emotions caused, I am able to re-run events like a video and decide in my mind to take any corrective action required after the event.
- *Midsight* (occurs after EI development). In the midst of events, I catch myself on the path heading downwards. I engage my thinking to salvage a better outcome. I stop the emotional reaction and its automatic behaviour, to be more in control.
- *Foresight* (occurs after a minimum of 21 days to a few months of EI development) comes from the 3rd Brain. Prior to interactions of any importance, I habitually manage my emotions and behaviour with people. I prepare for an emotionally intelligent outcome, consider the psychological process with people as much as the task.

Taking control of your behavioural patterns

We can train ourselves to react different, to react positively, and to use foresight rather than hindsight to manage our emotions. To be successful in this, we need to rehearse acquiring foresight frequently so that we become unconsciously competent in it. At this point we react in a different manner without really thinking about it. Just like switching on the lights of our new car without fumbling.

So, to manage our emotions we need to take control of our behaviours. To do that we must first recognise the emotional roots: certain behaviours are generally associated with specific emotions. For example, we approach people when we are enthusiastic, we sit around and do nothing when we are depressed and we fidget when anxious.

These are of course generalisations. If the behaviours go unchecked they perpetrate negative emotions. Often we don't notice our behaviour. A raised voice in response to anger or excitement means that we may not even be aware that we are doing it. If you want to change a situation of never or rarely being able to manage unhelpful emotions or impulses you are going to have to:

✓ understand the cost to you of the related anxiety and stress and decide that you do not want to pay this price any longer
✓ understand the triggers that are unique to you as an individual
✓ commit to more reflection on your behaviour. Initially, this will be with more hindsight but with practice you will catch yourself in the middle. Eventually you will achieve foresight about unhelpful impulses and bad habits before you act on them.

Becoming emotionally literate

Becoming able to label distinct emotions accurately allows us to examine the first time we experienced those emotions. Frequently, unhelpful behaviours in adults can be linked to interpretation during some past event. We experience a chain of emotions during an incident and we make it mean something about ourselves, about our standards or place in the world.

We use the fantasy level of self-awareness (3rd level, see Monday) to reinterpret the facts of the incident. We then bring the story into focus and the actual facts of what occurred fade into memory.

This interpretation is remembered and not the facts. It is carried through inappropriately into later life. This can be recycled many times and the story grows more distant from fact.

Exercising a new muscle

To develop your self-awareness you are going to develop a different part of your brain. It's like exercising a new muscle and it needs concentration. So to help you, here are a few very simple rules that you can apply quickly and easily.

- To express your thoughts start with the words, 'I think . . .'
- To express feelings, start with the words, 'I feel . . .', and then add a feeling word. If you say, 'I feel that . . .' then you are actually expressing what you think. Use the following table of emotions to expand your vocabulary of emotion-related adjectives.
- Essentially, we have just four primary feelings: Mad, Sad, Glad and Scared. However, we use many different words to describe them.
- Feelings can also be complex, known as blanket emotions, indicated by an asterisk (*) in the table. Some are composites of two or more primary feelings; e.g. jealousy can comprise envy, fear, sadness, sense of loss etc. If you are to sustain beneficial changes it is very important that you learn to distinguish the separate emotions involved in complex emotions. You must explore what might have originally triggered each one.

Recognising blanket emotions

MAD	SAD	GLAD	SCARED	OTHER
angry*	blue	amused	afraid	affectionate
annoyed*	depressed*	comfortable	agitated	bored*
ashamed	despondent	content	alone	closed
belittled*	discouraged	ecstatic	awkward	co-operative*
guilty	distressed	effervescent	concerned	dumb-founded*
irritated	down	elated	confused	loving
jealous*	down and out	excited	distressed	encouraged
disappointed	grief	fascinated	nervous	flummoxed*
discouraged	hurt	fulfilled	forgetful	forgiving
frustrated*	lonely	giddy	ignored*	fevered
furious*	left out	glorious	inhibited	guileful

We can use our increased personal insight and ability to
assess our feelings to revisit the first time these emotions
were experienced.

Emotional literacy exercise

Write down emotions that you are likely to experience
in your workplace: anger, joy, anxiety, contentment,
enthusiasm, fear, sadness and frustration.

- What behavioural patterns accompany the emotions
  that you are most likely to encounter at work?
- For all of the emotions on the list, what are your
  corresponding actions?
- Explore any unhelpful behavioural patterns. For
  example, you avoid running into your boss because
  you are afraid you might be moved from your job.

Look at your behavioural actions in response to other situations in your workplace. Visualising ourselves in the situation, we re-evaluate any negative self-beliefs that were formed or beliefs about others. We can then choose a new response to the chain of emotions triggered by the situation should we encounter them again.

Let me give you an example of a bad habit that I had before my EI coach helped me to distinguish where it came from.

Before EI development
I am away a lot in the course of my consultancy and training. The office equipment and software will be upgraded or replaced. When I get back, I need to allow time to catch up and learn to use it. Inevitably, I need to meet a deadline of some sort. However, I just want to use the office software and get on with completing things. Very often I have to ask for help because I make mistakes. My bad habit is being grumpy with the person who helps me.

Now, there is no logic in doing this and I wasn't very proud of myself for doing so. It is not rational to be difficult when someone is coming to your aid, nor was it something I planned to do or was aware I did.

During EI development
My EI coach suggested that I visualise being at the computer and at the point where I had to ask for help. He then persisted in asking me what my emotions were at the time.

I realised that I was angry but he did not let it rest there. Anger is a blanket emotion. The coach then asked about my past and if I could relate these emotions to anything. He framed it in such a way that I felt very adult about exploring it. It suddenly came to me that at a mainframe computer site where I had worked almost 20 years before, *I* used to be the person that people asked for expert help (on a particular computer language). I was not conscious of the impact on my self-esteem but clearly it had.

Let's look at the emotions concerning this, I felt:

- Jealousy – I am envious of the knowledge that whoever helps me has acquired
- Humiliated – I am the expert not the apprentice. I feel stupid on software that I have previously been very adept at using
- Resentful – I am out earning the money that paid for you (my helper) to gain this expertise
- Afraid – I am scared that I am getting out of touch and that I will never catch up
- Anger – I feel irritated and grumpy because of all the other feelings.

After EI development

Now, I appreciate that this is not a life-threatening situation and can appear trivial in the analysis. But the point is that I very quickly broke the bad habit and integrated the learning to look at other areas. On reflection, I was amazed at the range of emotions I had experienced.

The next time I started to get angry with the computer, my internal observer 'warning light' appeared in my head. I immediately felt amused instead of angry.

Sharing with my colleagues the trigger to the chain of emotions explained this mysterious behaviour to them. Since then I can have healthy adult-to-adult conversations about many behaviours, demonstrating to colleagues how they could use the EI coaching process for their own behavioural issues.

Moving from hindsight to foresight

From the EI coaching I learned to acquire foresight about potential emotional reactions, by going through a learning curve with time.

I felt really good about breaking these habits. This positive behaviour helped to reinforce the new behaviour. I had discarded the old neural pathway and built a new healthier one.

Competencies for self-control

The following competencies reflect my personal view of the
next step from self-awareness to self-control (although I am
aware that the role of emotion in behaviour is still being
examined with academic rigour).

**Self-regulation: Managing emotions and holding
back unhelpful impulses**

To have this competency you would:
- ❑ stop acting on impulse when it is an unproductive
  behaviour
- ❑ remain collected, positive and unflustered even at
  testing times
- ❑ manage distressing emotions and reduce anxiety
  associated with experiencing them
- ❑ think lucidly, remaining focused under pressure.

Authenticity: Being true to yourself and others

To have this competency you would:
- ❑ build trust through your reliability and congruent
  behaviour (words and actions are aligned)
- ❑ act ethically, being above reproach and questioning
  of your own motives
- ❑ admit flaws and confront unethical actions in others
  (zero tolerance)
- ❑ stand up for your values even when in the minority
- ❑ expect yourself to slip back occasionally and have a
  sense of humour and compassion about it.

Accountability: Taking responsibility, owning your performance

To have this competency you would:
- ❏ take responsibility for your actions and inaction where appropriate
- ❏ clear up miscommunication and keep promises
- ❏ hold yourself accountable to objectives
- ❏ prioritise what is important and urgent every day at work.

Flexibility: Embrace and adapt to change

To have this competency you would:
- ❏ take account of potential change in your planning
- ❏ be able to let go, accept shifting priorities and a challenging pace of change
- ❏ be adaptable in how you perceive events or different people
- ❏ be open to confronting change issues and exploring the personal implications
- ❏ be innovative to account for change, generating and sharing ideas.

Self-motivation: Positively managing your outlook

To have this competency you would:
- ❏ be driven to improve or meet high standards
- ❏ demonstrate commitment in all your relationships
- ❏ look for the opportunity first not the problem
- ❏ show persistence in pursuing goals and intentionality in overcoming barriers or setbacks.

If you tick everything in this competence, you have great emotional maturity. Developing a high EQ demands *accurate* self-assessment and *consistent* behaviour in all circumstances.

Journal entries and activities

You should ask a friend to review your strengths as a way to improve areas in which you are less capable. Remember that a generic goal of exercises is to learn the process of making small changes within your own limits. The purpose is not to be perfect. Be gentle with yourself if you are less than satisfied with the results.

Exercises to generate an Internal Observer
You need to practise deconstructing the emotional roots of your behaviour in routine work situations. The effectiveness of meetings and their impact on stress levels is mainly due to human relationships. Prepare by reflecting on past meetings, using the competencies described yesterday and today. Look at the agenda as early as possible. Routine meetings have packed agendas, however, you can still raise your self-awareness and self-control by using them as vehicles. Find out how other attendees regard agenda items in advance. You can explain that you are doing self-development to make meetings more valuable. Log insights from reflection in your journal:

- What happened
- Your feelings about it
- What went well
- What you would do differently.

Signs of low EQ to look for:

- Diversion – you are telling someone some details but become aware that some aspect of the communication triggers emotions, interfering with the message. For example, you become aware that your motive for this message is that you see this person achieving an unfulfilled ambition of yours
- Distraction – the body language of one or more attendees shows impatience and this is transmitted to you
- Internal dialogue – you drift off listening to your inner voice because some aspect of the here and now is of insufficient interest
- Interpretation – you make meeting occurrences mean something about you whereas in reality there is no personal inference at all
- Holding back or not contributing at all – these are indirect or passive aggressive behaviours
- Outrageous attention-seeking behaviour
- Using humour to avoid debating some real issue
- What hooks you and where do you go? You are confronted by something being acted out or said by participants. You retreat into self-denial, justification, avoidance or something else.

Tomorrow, we look at how developing your EI can be a significant contributor to your personal stress management strategies and practices.

Stress management and EI

Today, we are going to gain an understanding of the following topics:

- What is stress?
- Stress reactions
- Stress-related Illnesses
- Stress management strategies using EI
- Journal entries
- Stress audit

What is stress?

The word stress is derived from the Latin word 'stringere', which means to draw tight. According to Hinkle (1973), 'in the seventeenth century the word was used to describe hardship or affliction'.

As we discovered on Sunday, when threatened by a tiger, your body pumps in nor-adrenaline to prepare for fight or flight. Sugars, cholesterol and fatty acids are released into the bloodstream and blood pressure and heartbeat increase.

There is an immediate and powerful mood change; you do not start smiling or laughing in these circumstances. Primed for action, the nor-adrenaline surge is an 'upper' to optimise performance giving the best chance for short-term survival.

In general, people react badly with either too little or too much stress in the long term. Without some sense of challenge (eustress or 'good' stress sensed as exhilaration and excitement) we would not get out of bed. In everyday normal stressful situations, the experience is pleasurable because one survives the threat.

In basic terms, stress is an aspect of living that can be beneficial when it motivates, inspires or encourages change. It can be the opposite when it does not (distress); individuals perceive that they do not have the resources to cope with a perceived situation from the past, present or future.

Stress reactions

The 'stress' that people complain about is a feeling of tension or pressure experienced when demands placed upon them (Stressors) are perceived as exceeding the resources they have available.

The stress cycle
The fight or flight response has been well researched and monitored. It develops in the following cycle:

- the forebrain receives danger signals from eyes, ears etc.
- the hypothalamus, in the brain, activates the pituitary gland to release hormones
- Senses are activated, e.g. the pupils of the eyes dilate.
- Breathing rate increases and gets deeper. Heart rate and blood pressure increase
- The liver releases sugar, cholesterol and fatty acids into the blood stream
- Digestion ceases and bladder and bowel openings contract.
- The adrenal glands release hormones, adrenaline, nor-adrenaline and cortisone, which cause increased sweating and blood clotting ability.

The most common symptom is that people don't feel well and medical practitioners can find no clinical reason.

As we covered on Sunday, during the Stone Age there would have been physical activity in fighting or running and the danger would have passed quickly.

In the 21st century, the body response is the same but the threats we perceive are of a financial, emotional, mental and a social nature. These types of threats are constantly present in our environment and are not generally dealt with quickly.

Stress-related illnesses

Being constantly stressed causes illness because the metabolic change is continuous, preventing relaxation or proper sleep for the body and mind to repair itself. Some long-term effects can be: hair loss, headache, migraine, strokes, impaired immune response, nervousness, bad sleeping, neck and shoulder aches, lower back and leg ache, asthma, skin conditions, high blood pressure, bad circulation, heart diseases, some cancers, indigestion, ulcers, irritable bowel syndrome, impotency, menstrual disorders and rheumatoid arthritis. The negative effects of stress can also be visible in the form of bad decision-making, negative internal politics, reduced creativity and apathy.

If optimum performance is continually maintained or surpassed (chronic stress), then performance deteriorates rapidly and people eventually become ill or die. Chronic stress is a cumulative phenomenon that can develop over a lifetime or over a few weeks. A vicious circle or rather spiral is entered into with the stress response to fear driving an individual to produce more effort for less performance, with more time spent working and less in relaxation.

Often it is not the obvious 'stress-straw' that 'breaks the camel's back'. In the working environment, chronic stress often develops from a lifestyle encouraged by employers to gain short-term competitive advantage, which has, say, a bereavement 'straw' or house move added to it. Absenteeism generated by chronic stress can cause a 'domino' collapse of employees as each person experiences overload when coping with their own work and that of absent colleagues.

Work—life balance

How well do you believe you balance your time between work and play and family and employer? As often happens, if there are feelings that the balance is not right, some typical reasons may be:
- You enjoy the work
- You fear jeopardising your career
- You perceive that your boss expects it
- You endure a workaholic organisational culture
- You think that you have to prove you can cope.

Write up in your journal what you have discovered about your motivation for imbalances.

Whatever the pressures on you at work it is necessary to recognise the importance of relaxation and doing things that we enjoy.

Stress management strategies using EI

Because of the way an EI programme is structured (covered on Thursday and Friday), it allows people to build the skills to reduce stress on a continual basis. Returning to the programme outcomes every 3 months over a 1-year period enables progress to be reviewed. Developmental areas can be shared and from this, creative solutions generated. Working with a group rewards the new behaviours being instilled.

Like risk, stress is a perception and therefore highly personal. Here is a series of checklists of stress management measures, which, by managing what we cannot avoid and by eliminating what we can, will lead to better health.

- Manage your relationships
- Manage your environment
- Manage your lifestyle
- Manage your attitude or reactions.

Manage your relationships
- For one week log notes in your journal about changes to your stress levels depending on who you are with at the time.
- Have authentic, emotionally intelligent relationships with people. Associate with those whose company you enjoy and who support you. Authenticity requires self-awareness and emotional expression so that when in conversation with an individual you are able to share your feelings openly, including any distractions impairing your ability to concentrate on them. The relationship would be equitable and based on a sense of mutuality. While the degree of give and take may vary from time to time based on your needs, it would find an agreed equilibrium. When worries start to build up, talk to someone with whom you have a close relationship.
- Learn how to have assertive conversations with those who create anxiety by not acknowledging your feelings and rights. As much as possible, clear your life of people who drain your emotional battery creating unacceptable anxiety and conflict. Don't drift along in troublesome and distressing situations or relationships. Take action to change rather than trying to avoid the problem or

deny it exists. Taking chances is the key to emotional well-being.

- Protect your personal freedoms and space. Do what you want and feel, but respect the rights of others. Don't tell others what to do, but if they intrude, let them know.
- Set up a co-coaching relationship with someone you trust, preferably someone with coaching experience. Meet at least once a month, split the time and have a scheduled phone call every week. Select life-improving books to read and share together. Tackle real issues including denial and avoidance with each other. Use your journal entries and prepare for the co-coaching sessions, writing the results up at the time and after reflection. Note the advice on coaching in Friday's chapter.
- Watch your conversations for faulty thought patterns, such as selective envy, disaster forecasting, finding the scapegoat, generalisation and projecting our reactions onto others.

Manage your environment

For one week, log in your journal notes about changes to
your stress levels and the environment you are in at the time.

- Being ruthless, identify the Stressors and think what you
  can do about them (e.g. clutter in the house, shed and
  garage, or your journeys to work, or the lack of a study or
  'den' for you)
- Surround yourself with cues from positive thoughts and
  relaxation
- Find a time and place each day where you can have
  complete privacy. Take time off from others and pressures.

Manage your lifestyle

Change your lifestyle by removing the causes of stress. Look
at the following.

- Effective time management is just one of many ways to
  keep from succumbing to stress overload. Make time to
  learn and practise relaxation or meditation skills.
- Engage in a vigorous physical exercise that is convenient
  and pleasurable. Check with your doctor before engaging
  on a new programme if you are unused to it. Sometimes it
  helps to get a friend to exercise with you to keep the
  discipline. Go to a gym or fitness centre that has
  instructors with recognised qualifications. Always do their
  induction session.
- Short breaks during the day (every 45 minutes if
  working at a computer) can help improve efficiency and
  well-being the rest of the day. In addition, the breaks
  help with avoidance of problems with posture (lower
  back syndrome), eyesight and Repetitive Strain Injuries
  (RSI).

- Maintain a reasonable diet and sane sleeping habits. Use alcohol and medication wisely; you must be in control of them not vice versa. Avoid the use of sleeping pills, tranquillisers and other drugs to control stress (exercise really helps with sleeping problems as does a diet that acknowledges foods that can stimulate you throughout the day or encourage sleep at night.)

Manage your attitude

We are not upset by things but rather the view we take of them.   Epictetus

You may have a positive attitude to something that is causing you and others around you stress. It may be a weakness because of its extreme nature when it could be moderated and become a strength. Apart from the need to balance life and career, our personal characteristics play an important role in creating stress. Seek the view of others on the characteristics that might add to your stress, such as:

- perfectionism
- misdirected anxiety
- need for approval of others
- pessimism
- impatience
- a wish to avoid conflict
- poor opinion of self.

If we wish to avoid undue stress we must recognise the role such characteristics play and be prepared to modify our values. Reflect on this and write the results up in your journal.

Shortly, we will look at a stress audit that can start you on this programme as a diagnostic phase.

An EI approach to reducing stress
You might want to experiment to see what works best for you. The features of an emotionally intelligent approach that can tackle stress are:

- Increasing competencies in self-awareness, self-control and in awareness of others
- Viewing life as challenges to seek and not as obstacles to avoid. Review your obligations from time to time and make sure they are still good for you. If they're not, let them go
- Using assertiveness through a balance of responsive and assertive behaviours
- Identifying positive approaches to events, rather than just tormenting yourself with negative thoughts and emotions.
- Understanding the true cost of our values and beliefs
- Not becoming one-dimensional. Don't let one thing dominate you, such as a current project, schoolwork, relationships, career, sports, hobby etc.

- Opening yourself to fresh experiences; try new-fangled things, novel foods and new places; take responsibility for your life and your feelings, but never blame yourself. Ownership of your life is a better philosophy than a blame culture.

Journal entries

Using the definitions of self-awareness and self-control, explore how EQ competencies can help you. Record thoughts in your journal after completion of the stress audit. This allows you to assess the impact of raising EQ on stress-reduction.

Reflection exercise

Pick out some competencies for self-control (from Tuesday) that you want to develop. Look at some strength that you want to use more. Think of routine events in the next 2 weeks that you can use to develop them. Set yourself some **smart** objectives (**s**pecific, **m**easurable, **a**ction-orientated, **r**ealistic and **t**ime-boxed). After 2 weeks, ask the following questions in self-study or with a friend or colleague.

- What was the single most challenging thing in the last 2 weeks about your behaviour change?
- What obstacles were there to stop you accomplishing your daily goals?
- Did the same distraction keep coming up or were the obstacles different each time?
- What helped you to succeed? What was the easiest thing for you in the last 2 weeks about your behaviour change?

- Did you know this about yourself before you began?
- Was there a time when you struggled with your goal? Record what day it was. What else was going on?
- How did you bring yourself back into the 'here and now'? Can you do this at will?
- What was difficult about letting go of old behaviours – was there some pay-off in them for you? Did your internal observer talk to you and did you ignore the messages?

Write down the answers to the following questions:

- How do you see yourself at your best (e.g. if you are a perfectionist, you may be driving yourself too hard, striving for the impossible)?
- What, in the past 12 months, was the most challenging or exciting event in my life?
- In the past 12 months, which of the following event(s) was/were quite stressful?

Stress audit

Write down the answers to the following questions in your journal:
- Do you ever feel unable to cope?
- Do you find it difficult to relax?
- Do you ever feel anxious for no reason?
- Do you find it hard to show your true feelings?
- Are you finding it hard to make decisions?

- Are you often irritable for no reason?
- Do you worry about the future?
- Do you feel isolated and misunderstood?
- Do you doubt that you like yourself?
- Are you finding it difficult to concentrate?
- Do you find that life has lost its sparkle?
- I believe that for me stress is . . .
- Some Stressors in my life are:
  - ❑ Life pressures
  - ❑ Satisfaction with life
  - ❑ General health and fitness
  - ❑ Quality of life
  - ❑ Relationships

Review previous entries to see what is related. Carry the learning from one over to the other. You may find some barriers to learning or resistance to change.

Tomorrow we are taking EI development into the workplace for the whole organisation.

What will my company gain from an investment in EI?

Today, we are going to gain an understanding of the following topics:

Investment in EI
How to create an EI culture:

- EI culture change project life cycle
- Stage 1: Creating the EI team
- Stage 2: Diagnosing and exploring change in
  your organisation
- Stage 3: Closure of issues
Journal entries
- Actions to ensure success

Investment in EI

Many people have a passion to reinvent their organisation. I suggest here that creating an EI culture can be part of that reinvention. If you want to change the world, start by changing yourself. 'You have to **be** the change you wish for the world' (Gandhi). Firstly, let's understand the business context by looking at a common scenario. In the 20th century, HR specialists sought:

- to produce measures that help the frontline to do anything faster, better, cheaper; or
- to produce measures that are clear enablers, neither barriers nor things that hamper operations.

You also have to generate differentiating products and services. However, I believe an EI culture can remove the friction that holds you back and can provide emotional stamina to tackle global challenges.

HR people will be faced with leaders who hire people solely for knowledge and task-orientation, not their 'way of being' skills with customers, suppliers and colleagues. Does this sound familiar to you?

I believe that EI will define success in the 21st century, *doing* more will not be enough – *being* different might achieve the highest goals.

We lose customers as well as staff for EQ-related reasons. In other words, we deliver superior products but the service aspect is lacking in some way. Let's look at the economics of this if you feel disinclined to spend money on remedial work.

It is 16 times cheaper to sell another product or service to an existing customer than to find a new client. It makes hard cash sense to expend effort in not only retaining existing satisfied customers but in converting them to advocates. Creating advocacy brings an average of five new customers at very low cost of acquisition.

A dissatisfied customer will tell three times more people about you than an advocate. Fifteen people will be put off using your product or service – that is very expensive.

DEPARTMENT STORE

How is this related to improvements in EQ? If the cause of complaint is explored and the customer handled using great self-control, awareness and influencing skills a transformation can be achieved – even a conversion to an advocate. The collection of high-quality and comprehensive information for marketing and R&D purposes also requires excellent social skills and awareness of others.

The cost of low EQ

Think back to Sunday and the three incidents involving a customer/supplier relationship.
- Think back to the exchanges between people
- Have a go at looking at the costs involved in the outcome
- Can you see that higher EQ here can lead to sustainable, profitable relationships with customers and cheaper customer acquisition?
- What would this look like for your company?

Positive affirmation – a milestone in an Emotionally Intelligent culture

One of the ways to **be** different is to bring up a child to be an emotionally intelligent adult using positive affirmation. Without this, the emergent adult will be without the skills at work to generate and participate in a beneficial climate.

The reasons why the practice of positive affirmation is a milestone in an emotionally intelligent culture are:

- It brings rewards, such as netting undiscovered potential, into the workplace
- It allows teams to celebrate more and be positive with a regular sense of well-being
- It avoids the language of human deficit that blocks cultures like cholesterol clogs arteries
- Combined with heightened emotional states and other techniques designed to take advantage of brain function, positive affirmation can be embedded in one instance of learning (it does not have to be repeated many times to stick).

Consider the above bullets and come up with ideas on how to achieve them. Record in your journal your reaction to your answers and any thoughts regarding them.

People are not naturally prone to giving positive feedback (Wheldall and Merrett). This varies from culture to culture and it may strike more of a note with you. Adults need to be educated to unlearn years of being covertly rewarded for cutting people down to size. Working in a culture that does not positively re-enforce, feedback becomes associated solely with negative comments. In this climate, praise is given in a vacuum of detail. Criticism is remembered with 20/20 vision *forever*.

For praise to achieve its aim there is a requirement to give specific evaluative feedback. This lets people know what they have done in particular, so that good behaviours become ingrained. However, it is not unusual for managers to overplay the 'exceeds expectations' grading in performance appraisals due to fear of accurate feedback being construed as unsupported criticism. On the occasions that positive feedback is given, it is not given rigorously and systematically, i.e. in a way that is going to change people's behaviour. To change the adult, you may have to revisit the child within:

- the climate in which they were brought up,
- which behaviours were rewarded and how overtly or covertly
- which behaviours were punished.

How to create an EI culture

In this and the next chapter, we are going to look at how to create an EI culture.

EI culture change project life cycle
A typical life cycle for an EI culture change project has the following stages (run in parallel to some degree using different resources):

Stage 1: Creating the EI team
Stage 2: Diagnosing and exploring change
Stage 3: Closure of issues surrounding the old culture and discovering the new culture
Stage 4: Two-way communication of the dream or vision for the new culture
Stage 5: Designing a programme to deliver the dream or vision, including what has to be given up
Stage 6: Piloting the design pragmatically
Stage 7: Reviewing the pilot and matching the results against expectations
Stage 8: Completing the cycle for the rest of the organisation
Stage 9: Activities and practices sustaining the results.

Stage 1: Creating the EI team

With businesses under pressure financially and competitively, it is not a good idea to utilise consultants on repeated activities that could be done by internal or specialist staff after they have been given extra capabilities. To be economic, a 'Forest Fire' approach is expedient (starts from a point selected by external experts and is spread outwards by a handpicked internal EI team).

The EI team is composed of those with good facilitation skills and an affiliative approach, selected from:

- the Organisational Development team
- HR or Training and Development teams
- volunteers – inspired individuals dedicated to reinventing the organisation (but check how you are going to select them for suitability)
- external consultants hired for expertise to transfer knowledge and skills by training and coaching the internal EI team.

The EI team members may need to go through a formal assessment process to get the mix right for the programme. The skills of these individuals could be raised by a number of interventions: coaching and assessment, paired facilitation of others, regular feedback and Continuous Professional Development (CPD).

If available funding is extremely low, a bespoke Train The EI Coach course can be developed and delivered by the HR Manager (or project sponsor if that role is going to be very hands-on). This course should include how to evaluate the potential of the EI team back in their new role.

Developed to become resilient EI change agents and coaches, members must be able to cope well with participants enduring the agonies of raising themselves through the learning ladder (see Sunday). During workshop sessions, specific change issues will impact participants' lives. They will be confronted by what it means for them to meet the new demands of the business.

Rolling it out as a pilot programme, the EI team would transfer change agency to managers and staff as quickly as possible with expert guidance as required.

After creating the EI team, I recommend that you begin with a diagnostic phase in order to understand the current organisational culture. This provides an opportunity to finalise the way forward.

Stage 2: Diagnosing and exploring change in your organisation

Run through the tick list below thinking about your current organisation. Which of them can you tick without any doubts in your mind?

Organisational checklist

❑ My organisation has a strategic view

❑ Senior people energise others lower in the system

❑ Leaders here create a structure that follows function

❑ Managers make decisions at a point when the relevant information is held or comes together

---

❑ This company has a reward system that balances what you know and what you do

❑ We have relatively open communication

❑ We reward collaboration when it is in the organisation's best interests

❑ Our managers manage conflict, they do not suppress it

❑ Our leaders view the organisation as an open system and manage the demands put upon it

❑ Our organisation values individuality and individuals

❑ We actively learn through feedback

The above checklist is part of a Healthy Organisation Checklist by Beckhard in his work. *Organisational Transitions – Managing Complex Change*. The more ticks indicates the greater health of your organisation. Record in your journal your reaction to each answer and any thoughts regarding reinvention. You could consider the above checklist to be a series of milestones for entry into a change management plan for the EI culture change project.

If you have ticked all of them then you are fortunate to work in an organisation that is emotionally literate and shares learning. I recommend that you share the checklist with as many people as possible to come up with a joint diagnosis. You will be unable to mobilise people to change without such agreement.

Diagnosing change

- Thinking about change in your organisation, what kind of change do you want in the following areas?

> Organisational policies
> Leadership styles
> Environment
> Relationships
> Processes, procedures or practices
> Attitudes
> Behaviour.

- For each of the above, who needs to be involved?
- How ready or fit for change is your organisation?
- How prepared is it for the changes you want?
- Who or what are the forces for and against the changes?
- How realistic are the changes you want?
- How can you modify your change needs to make them more realistic?
- What resources can you tap into?

> Help from Government, such as grants, cheap loans, agencies and business schemes?
> Central resources as part of a group or larger organisation?
> Internal teams set up for this purpose?
> Volunteers? How will you measure their suitability?

- Thinking of your organisation at present:

> Which part is most vulnerable to change from external drivers?
> Which part is most vulnerable to change from internal drivers?

Record the answers in your journal. If you do not know the answers then enquire into how a change process might be initiated in your organisation. People often feel safer doing some exploration about what change would feel like and how it could happen. See Stage 3 as mandatory if you are in this situation.

Stage 3: Closure of issues

For the want of a stage like this, many culture change programmes fail to achieve a critical mass of transformation. To generate an EI culture, it is vital for staff to let go of allegiance to the previous culture. There may be a good deal to give up in the way of unproductive behaviours, to which work-based teams are attached (albeit unknowingly). You need to discover what values people are wedded to on a daily basis and how they compare with any new values.

If they sense you view the old culture as wrong and the reason for moving forward is to put things right, this does not give credit for what has worked. Many people may have taken to heart a previous mission, vision and values. Start with praise of what has been achieved to date to show respect, and to translate the success to the new paradigm collaboratively through skilled facilitation. In addition, it is vital that the reward and remuneration mechanisms are updated to incentivise the new behaviours.

Common business scenarios are of mergers or acquisitions where programmes are initiated in the shadow of earlier ones. People may feel that previous work goes unrecognised, and this may stop them supporting the new ideas and methods. They may not even be aware of previous beliefs and actions; it is possible for cultures to be implicit rather than explicit.

In order for staff to alter both attitudes and behaviour, they need to understand 'What's in it for me'. Research shows that without this understanding people may *appear* to change without fundamentally altering their attitudes or behaviour. It is safer for them to stay where they are in terms of mindset, not to buy in or even for people to sabotage the new culture. There is always a payoff for behaving in these ways, such as:

- Getting to be right
- Playing the cynic and never having to commit to anything
- Dominating or bullying others
- Self-justification
- Blaming others and not being responsible
- Martyrdom – professional victims frequently switch places and persecute their victimiser.

What is needed is to be clear about the present culture, lay it to rest, and model the new. Without this, fundamental step change will not occur.

Regenerate enthusiasm for the organisation moving onto the next stage by checking the sense of 'permission to proceed'. The permission status may be manifest in hard management decisions on financial approvals for change consultancy or for staff being released from operations for change events.

It is essentially a contracting issue for the EI team whose mission it is to change the organisation with those who officially (and unofficially) hold sway in the organisation. We'll continue these stages tomorrow.

Journal entries

Study the following actions to ensure success and make notes in your journal on how they apply to your organisation.

Actions to ensure success
1 Make sure that employees are clear about the previous culture
2 Celebrate the past achievements by providing opportunities for them to feel acknowledged for what they've done well
3 Avoid any elitism of the Executive having higher paid coaches than the workforce.

Today, we have examined the creation of the EI Team responsible for change agency. We have looked at the ways to diagnose and explore necessary changes. In addition, we have determined the need for closure on past ways and respect for what has been achieved. Tomorrow, we move on to look at implementation.

How to create an EI culture

Continuing from Thursday, today we are going to explore
how to create an EI culture as follows:

> How to create an EI culture
> – Stage 4:   Two-way communication
> – Stage 5:   Designing a programme
> – Stage 6:   Piloting the design pragmatically
> – Stage 7:   Reviewing the pilot
> – Stage 8:   Completing the cycle
>
> Journal entries
> –   Learning organisation mind map
> –   Programme outcomes

Stage 4: Two-way communication

The communication of the dream or vision for the new EI
culture must be effective both ways reporting from top to
bottom and vice versa:

- The strategy must enrol all staff in the new approach
  clearly stating the benefits, including financial ones, and
  speculative risks
- The strategy must ensure that there is sponsorship of the
  new culture by those with power in the organisation.

Actively increase 'shop floor' participation using skills
transferred from change agents. Plan to reduce over time the
scale of intervention by change agents, managers, consultants

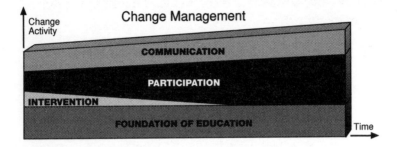

or trainers. Do not reduce the effort for Continuous Professional Development, education or communication.

It is often economic to bring in experienced executives who can model the new behaviours and it is not unusual for senior executives who cannot to elect to leave.

Stage 5: Designing a programme

A culture change project should start with a self-awareness programme (Step 1 overleaf). If members of staff are not able to see themselves as others see them, it is pointless attempting to raise their social skills and awareness of others. The design must include what has to be given up to achieve the dream or vision.

The five-step EI team programme
For the EI team, I recommend a five-step training and development process laid out below. I would suggest that a pivotal goal is that the EI team creates a 'critical mass' of advocates and exemplars of the new culture. It is essential that this programme be considered a business priority. The whole company should be put through as many of the steps

as can be afforded with a recommended minimum of the
two marked with an asterisk.

Step 1 ***Foundation** (see Monday) – Self-awareness and
knowledge about own EI competencies – Awareness
of feelings, Personal insight and self-assurance.
Identification of a first set of unproductive
behaviours and commitment to change through
development back in the workplace.

Step 2 ***Generating an Internal Observer** (see Tuesday) –
Using increased self-awareness from Step 1 to
increase self-control by identifying the emotional
triggers to unproductive behaviour – enhancing Self-
regulation, Authenticity, Accountability, Flexibility
and Self-motivation.

Step 3 **Change agency and stress management** (see
Wednesday) – Using Steps 1 and 2 to understand
sources of stress, to generate and commit to stress
management strategies. To understand and utilise
change management techniques suitable for self, use
with others and organisationally.

Step 4 **Conflict management, negotiation and assertive
behaviour** – Influencing strategies and techniques are
explored to resolve conflict equitably, to reconcile
differences in negotiations and to practise assertive
behaviour.

Step 5 **Developing specific EI coaching skills using a
seven-step coaching process and method** (see
Effective Coaching by Marshall J Cook (McGraw Hill)).

5.1 **Contracting phase** – The challenge faced by the

coachee and the required outcome are identified. The contract for the coaching relationship is explored and the commitment is made.

5.2 **The coaching approach** - Possible approaches to the coaching process are brainstormed based on understanding of the context of the challenge as well as the employees' personal issues. Lateral thinking is encouraged and unconventional ideas given consideration.

5.3 **The action plan** - The first meeting needs to complete some time management and the practical aspects of the coaching environment. What type of environment is suitable to the nature of the challenge (complete privacy needed or relative privacy of noisy public venue)? What aids might be needed if any?

5.4 **Agree deadlines** - What is the schedule and arrangements for changing it (revisit contract if required)?

5.5 **Evaluation** - What are the criteria for evaluation of success? How will the coachee know when the coaching is working? When will the coach establish that his or her subject is not coachable on this topic?

5.6 **Facilitate action** – What can you as coach do to help your employees succeed? Facilitation involves avoiding being tempted to rescue employees, thus stealing their autonomy of action and thought. Paternalistic or maternalistic approaches that take over the task from the employee are diametrically opposed to the coaching approach.

5.7 **Follow through** – This is a collaborative way of enforcing deadlines and setting time to review progress to ensure well-intentioned plans do not get lost.

Working with the executive layer, the programme may be re-iterated with the first batch becoming 'super coaches'. Coherent management of the change programme can be achieved by merging EI competencies with hard managerial and analytical skills.

EI learning methodology
The programme should generate opportunities for experiential learning, sharing knowledge of EI and change agency.

Classroom-based work
By being very interactive, participants practise the skills they are developing through a variety of training methods, which meet delegates' varying learning styles:

- a variety of accelerated learning techniques and exercises to help practise new skills and knowledge
- Mind Mapping[TM] or Freenoting[R] to speed learning and ensure thorough understanding of the new concepts
- presentation and discussion of relevant material and debate to facilitate understanding of their role in the organisation
- Self/peer evaluated role-plays to allow delegates to practise skills and to facilitate self-assessment of their own developing skills
- activities allowing delegates to understand themselves and the ways they interact with others, e.g. games to understand how they relate to colleagues and customers (both internal and external), or team building exercises to facilitate support of each other in their new role.

Development at work
Working with the business to embed EI coaching in the culture and processes, developmental learning back at work should be provided to ensure success within the work context. Exercises should be designed to fit in with routine events in the workplace, e.g. team meetings. This will include the following:

- focus groups or workshops, e.g. ways of developing structures to generate the EI programme internally
- directed self-study and shared EI exercises
- learning sets and cross-functional teams

- facilitated e-rooms to share knowledge and experience (if you have the technology and are globally disparate)
- one-to-one coaching or supervised/observed coaching sessions or team coaching.

Learning outcomes for EI culture change interventions
People behave as they are rewarded. Organisations waste money by charging ahead with training while delaying alignment of reward mechanisms to the learning outcomes. This is essential in Stage 5. Mismatches are very disillusioning for participants. Once you know what hard performance indicators and behavioural competencies are required, you must act on this.

In order for participants to continue to adopt a positive approach throughout the organisation, it is important that they have coaching immediately following each course. It would be helpful if their consolidation successes are recognised (rewards, reviews, appraisal etc).

Learning outcomes of the five-step programme

By the end of the programme, the EI team will have achieved all the learning outcomes:

- Have a sense of self-esteem and self-confidence and the ability to maintain them under all circumstances – successfully managing themselves in challenging situations
- Further develop a variety of interpersonal skills, e.g. assertiveness, managing their own emotional responses, rapport building etc.
- Display integrity, honesty and authenticity, when dealing with colleagues, creating more effective teams
- Be able to recognise when they relate to people using their previous opinions rather than looking for opportunities to reinforce new behaviours
- Have measured their approach to feedback and discussed the present organisational culture
- Understand how to use positive feedback in order to change behaviour
- Improve their strategies to consistently generate positive feedback
- Be able to self-assess their positive feedback to employees
- Understand the purpose of EI coaching and analyse their strengths and areas of development as coaches
- Respect the autonomy of coachees in action and thought
- Use a variety of coaching styles and understand when a particular approach is required, e.g. more direction
- Set up structures that facilitate an enduring coaching culture which boosts sales, stimulates creativity and engenders co-operation

Stage 6: Piloting the design pragmatically

Do not select the worst region because you want to change it
the most and think that this will form a useful pilot. Your
consultant team may well be experienced enough to tackle
this region but your new EI coaches may find it too big a
step. This will be demoralising and you need to start with a
winner. In surrounding regions that have taken the
transformation well and have emotional stamina, you can
always restructure (each absorbing parts of the difficult
region) using the critical mass.

Make sure that you have consulted all stakeholders on the
pilot evaluation criteria. Be clear that you know what good
looks like in the new behavioural competencies in the
opinion of all the key decision-makers. To sustain the new
culture it is essential that those who will judge competence
are reliable and consistent.

Usually consultants 'start the fire' and teach others how to
spread it with a wedge of resources that reduces with time.
The goal is for the EI team to transfer all of their knowledge
and skills to the business through experiential learning. The
approach will only be successful if the recipients pick up all
of the skills needed from the consultants and do not dilute
the messages.

It is wise for the EI team to remain ahead of the learning
curve to maintain a gap between them and the main body of
personnel. They are then able to support staff stopping any
cultural shear between workers, supervisors, middle
managers and the executive level.

During the transition phase, EI team members would be
coached to ensure that they have understood the models,

practice and experience of EI coaching. The transition phase would be to complete the transfer of knowledge. Evaluation would be a continuous process, thereby ensuring business needs are met.

The pilot would then be used to decide to what scale external support remains necessary and to complete the implementation plan for the wider organisation based on success.

Stage 7: Reviewing the pilot

Reviewing the pilot and matching the results against expectations, I would not expect to see financial pay back in less than 12 months. However, within 3 months I would expect individuals to evidence and report personal perceptions of benefit. They may be able to quote specific examples where use of their new EI competencies generated new business, protected existing business, increased sales, or increased advocacy, e.g. handling customer complaints.

Stage 8: Completing the cycle

Completing the cycle for the rest of the organisation is vital. However, there are too many variables to give detailed advice here other than some general guidelines.

- Have a communications strategy right from the start which uses formal and informal chains of communication.
- Plan the change programme professionally paying equal attention to the psychological process that people will go through, as you do to the tasks, goals and techniques employed.

- Ideally, everyone in the company should receive at least the first two courses concentrating on achieving heightened self-awareness and a capability to use this awareness to increase self-control. Each of these should then be followed by a period of development back in the workplace.
- Put first-line supervisors through the programme first if you have to limit the volume. You can afford to leave middle management until quite late but not executives, specialists or first-line supervisors as they generate more risk if they are living the old culture.
- Have a feedback loop that evaluates comments from participants carefully, remembering where they are on the learning ladder. Participants can kick out at trainers and change agents when the subject matter is confronting because it is below their level of self-awareness (they do not know what they do not know). Anticipate this and have change techniques to hand, being prepared to give individuals extra coaching (refer back to the five-step course for the EI team).
- Do not be surprised if strong bonds emerge between the EI coaches and participants on their courses. Collaborative approaches between first line supervisors and the EI team will make the transition back to work seamless. Make the transition work by a process of encouraging supervisors to coach people emerging from courses, and by the EI team coaching the supervisors.
- Complete risk management exercises at three levels: business (speculative or good risks where you are speculating to accumulate), programme level (where many projects interact and are dependent) and the individual project level where they vary depending on the nature (Information System, building move, training lifecycle).

Key influencers and leaders in the business must reinforce the new culture. Methods of continuing the development of the organisation were included in the learning methodology in Stage 5.

Competency Assessment
By adopting a coaching style of leadership, managers both motivate employees to work harder and generate a more positive culture. This also facilitates retention of key staff. Using competency assessment techniques will support continuous improvement of operations:

- discriminating competencies – that separate superior performers from average performers
- core competencies – characteristics that a sample of people in a job would have in common and those that are needed to get the basic job done.

The coach can spread discriminating competencies from one individual (say high cross-sales results due to excellent questioning skills) across the team. Thus over time, yesterday's core competencies evolve based on the observed discriminating competencies of today. New joiners will be selected on the basis of the higher standard. The overall standard of the team rises with time, based on this learning cycle of continuous improvement.

Journal entries

Consider the following diagram. I believe that the EI programme can go a long way towards achieving the advantages of being a learning organisation. In your journal, taking a clockwise scan around the mind map, reflect on:

- where your organisation is at present
- where it wants to be and by when
- how it might get there.

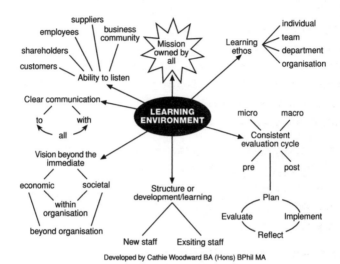

Developed by Cathie Woodward BA (Hons) BPhil MA

Develop a range of programme outcomes that you would like to achieve and incorporate these into a plan.

Today, we have completed how to create an EI culture. You should have enough information to work with internal teams and consultants on your own programme. Tomorrow, we are going to review the week developing a Personal Development Plan based on what we have learned.

Preparing for the next developmental steps

Today, we are going to explore what you might do after completing this book, by gaining an understanding of the following topics:

- The value of keeping a journal
- What a Personal Development Plan is and why it is useful
- Guidelines for completing a professional development analysis
- Designing a programme for you
- Steps in development

The value of keeping a journal

On Sunday, we covered the format for a journal entry and some experience concerning the value of doing so. The idea of keeping a journal is to consistently log your learning, keeping the information in one place readily to hand, and thus making it as easy as possible to do this. Alternatively, use the following formats and keep the logs in your Personal Development Plan folder:

- Learning log questionnaire
- Emotional Intelligence exercise log.

Learning log questionnaire
Give details of your role at that time and whether you are being supervised in these activities. Then record answers to the following bullets:

- Learning goals being worked on

- Record of the last exercise completed

- What learning occurred?

- List your main strengths and weaknesses during the exercise

- What learning goals do you wish to continue working on?

- Other comments.

Emotional Intelligence exercise log
Create a simple four-column table:

Exercise number	Date completed	With whom	Remarks

Leave whole rows between the exercises, so you can repeat each exercise with different people.

What a Personal Development Plan is and why it is useful

A PDP should start with a baseline entry developed using some techniques, such as a professional development analysis. Guidelines are given for this below. The PDP should be maintained throughout training. If possible, it can be updated every day using the learning outcomes, session objectives or teaching points as a structure. Personal development progress should be judged against agreed criteria for every job. Any gaps identified can be developed through a variety of methods, such as coaching and formal learning events. The choices available have been described earlier in the week.

If your organisation conducts 360° appraisals feeding into your PDP, try to keep the identification of gaps in a positive framework. If it becomes known that this process is always used to elicit weaknesses that are used in performance-related pay, then the shared insights will become defensive in nature. This will prevent a healthy learning pattern forming.

Guidelines for completing a professional development analysis

SWOT

To start a professional development analysis, you need to complete a SWOT (Strengths/Weaknesses/Opportunities/ Threats) table of four quadrants which considers:

- Internal – Strengths and Weaknesses – Consider these in specialist, technical and business skills and personal effectiveness (your EI competencies).
- External – Opportunities and Threats – Consider the impact of environmental drivers and personal factors including lifestyle plans.

You might like to consider those areas of weakness important to the business or to you personally. Similarly in respect of your strengths, there may be a business opportunity that requires you to develop one or more of these further, i.e. to expert level. Strengths and weaknesses must be considered in the light of the opportunities and threats.

Competency analysis

This involves identifying those capabilities required for a job or future aspiration. Identify the skills, knowledge and experience that are required to successfully meet the current and future requirements of your role and record them in a table such as this:

Competency analysis table				
Skills, knowledge and experience required for job or future aspirations	Important/ urgent	Current level 1–5	Target level 1–5	Gap description and size

Important/urgent grading

Score each skill according to its importance and urgency. Recognise what motivates you and expect it to have a higher priority. However, you may decide that a skill is less important but as part of personal growth you still wish to give it a high priority.

In addition to the above imperatives, identify those skills you might like to develop that will enrich or broaden you professionally and personally.

Competency – current level and target level

Grade your current level of competencey on a scale of 1–5 and then define the target level that you would like to achieve.

5 (Expert) – Practising at a level of excellence with high degree of skill and vast knowledge base

4 (Practitioner) – Proficient and above minimum standard required due to experience and advanced knowledge

3 (Foundation) – Meets minimum standard of competence, familiar and able to use relevant knowledge and skill

2 (Basic) – Some or little knowledge/skill, but unable to practise at a competent level

1 (Novice) – No knowledge/skill, requires extensive training.

Gap

Having identified your current and target level of competence, calculate the difference between the two levels. This figure will help you form a basis to identify those aspects that require professional development.

Summary

Having completed the SWOT and competency analyses consider those skills areas requiring development, taking into consideration:

- the scale of gap based on the analysis of your skills, experience and knowledge
- how important, urgent or critical they are to your current role or future aspirations.

Break down any large gaps into stages to make them manageable. Be realistic and identify what is achievable to be motivating. Consider further self-appraisal and feedback from clients, colleagues, mentors and others on your behaviour and emotional knowledge.

Designing a programme for you

To design a programme for you, you need to understand your learning preferences and prejudices. Skills and knowledge are usually acquired through training interventions away from work and on-the-job training. In addition you can ask to be given real organisational issues to tackle as projects to acquire experience and broaden your development. Development options include self-study, learning sets, cross-functional teams, and through use of learning technologies.

From Sunday you will appreciate that raising EQ is possible because EI is learnable. Complete a Learning Styles assessment to determine your tendencies. (Try www.peterhoney.com for his Learning Series.)

Expect to have two styles that predominate activity to round off your learning style to include all four behavioural patterns. This means that you are processing information and learning most comprehensively. It will save you a lot of time in the medium to long term.

Steps in development

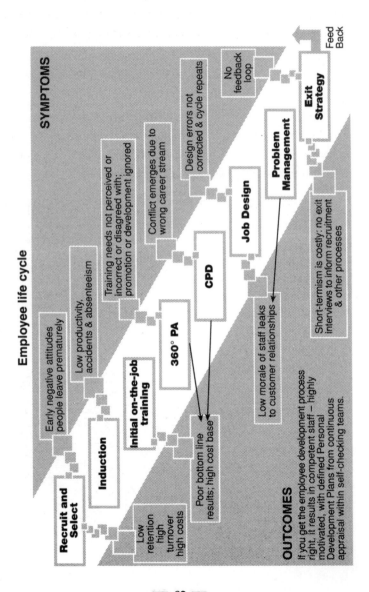

Employee life cycle

SYMPTOMS

Feed Back

- No feedback loop
- Design errors not corrected & cycle repeats
- Conflict emerges due to wrong career stream
- Training needs not perceived or incorrect or disagreed with; promotion or development ignored
- Low productivity, accidents & absenteeism
- Early negative attitudes people leave prematurely

Exit Strategy

Problem Management

Job Design

CPD

360° PA

Initial on-the-job training

Induction

Recruit and Select

- Short-termism is costly; no exit interviews to inform recruitment & other processes
- Low morale of staff leaks to customer relationships
- Poor bottom line results; high cost base
- Low retention high turnover high costs

OUTCOMES

If you get the employee development process right, it results in competent staff – highly motivated, with defined Personal Development Plans from continuous appraisal within self-checking teams.

Follow the employee life cycle, which illustrates symptoms of mismatches and unwanted outcomes. You should start your PDP on joining your first organisation. Update it at every life cycle step for the rest of your career. Example of PDP entries:

1. Induction and initial business training
2. On-the-job rehearsal (sitting-next-to-Nelly)
3. Coaching sessions
4. Continuous learning through Continuous Professional Development, including structures for developing further line responsibility by embedding reward and remuneration into the process
5. Learning sets and cross-functional teams with validation of materials and accreditation of individual's learning by an appropriate academic institution
6. Two-way communication between your own company and other global brand leaders to maximise learning.

Creating a structure – prepare, conduct, reflect

Experience of running EI programmes has led me to the conclusion that inviting people to carry out further tasks after training is futile. Even the most careful contracting in the world is challenged by people's return to work. I suggest a more lateral approach:

- improve the work environment to make learning a part of your business as usual
- make doing development activities a way of preparing for, conducting and reflecting on routine events at work.

Use the EI development exercises contained in this book to prepare, conduct and reflect on everyday events. The concept is that your way of 'being' will be different, rather than the way you use techniques or are driven by your task-orientation. Plan to run exercises utilising as many relationships as possible seeking collaboration with others and using the book to set the context if others are anxious or confused.

Emotions are not merely the remnant of our pre-sapient past but rather they form important characteristics of an active, searching and thinking human being. Anything that is a novelty, a discrepancy or an interruption generates a visceral response, while our cognitive system interprets the world as threatening, exciting, frightening or joyful.

The human world is so replete with emotions, not because we are animals at heart, but because it is so full of things that elate or threaten us. With new research into the nature of emotional experience and expression, it is possible to enquire into the role of emotions in adaptive behaviour. Consider that your successors may be the result of a new form of Natural Selection.

- If Darwin was right, what will be the process of Natural Selection for humans in the 21st century and will Emotional Intelligence have been a positive selection factor? Selection might be based upon those able to manage the stresses without unbalancing mind and body; the 100-hour long office jungle; commuting and supermarket shopping in the peak period: extended school holidays; and other aspects of everyday 21st century life.
- Of those organisations that adapt to survive, which will endure and why?

I hope that you will conclude (as I did) that, once started, developing your EQ becomes a life-long enquiry into the joys and mysteries of being human.

For information

on other

IN A **WEEK** titles

go to

www.inaweek.co.uk